Medieval Britain

S. L. Case & D. J. Hall

Illustrated by Brian Allen

Bell & Hyman
London

Published in 1983 by BELL & HYMAN LIMITED
Denmark House, 37–39 Queen Elizabeth Street, London SE1 2QB

First published in 1972 by Evans Brothers Limited
Reprinted 1973, 1974, 1975, 1976, 1977, 1979 (twice), 1981, 1984

Acknowledgements
Department of the Environment pp. 11, 12, 18, 40
Aerofilms Ltd. p. 16
Lady Magnus-Allcroft p. 22
York City Department of Tourism p. 17
Trustees of the British Museum p. 32
Thomas photos p. 34
Mansell collection p. 42
National Portrait Gallery p. 46
Stills from 'Henry V' and 'El Cid' by courtesy of
The Rank Organisation Limited pp. 38, 44, 26
Still from 'King Lear' by courtesy of
Columbia Pictures Corporation Ltd. p. 28
Camera Press Ltd. p. 27

ISBN 0 7135 2421 9

Filmset and printed by
BAS Printers Limited, Over Wallop, Hampshire

Contents

How to use this book

In this book you will find lots of information about life in the Middle Ages. Some of the information is written down for you to read and some of it is in pictures. Study the pictures very carefully because they will tell you a great deal about life in those days.

In this book you will also find lots of things to do. Sometimes you will be asked to write things in your own words, sometimes to copy and fill in blank spaces and sometimes to draw. All the things to do in your exercise book (or if you like in a separate scrapbook) are printed in heavy type like this:

Things to do.

When you do the exercises you will sometimes need some help. You will find the words to help you in boxes like this:

Words to help you.

If you decide to do the exercises on paper and stick them into a scrapbook you can collect pictures and postcards of the things you write about and put those into your scrapbook as well. In this way you can make a book about the Middle Ages which would be nice to keep. Your teacher will tell you where to write for pictures from museums but you will probably find lots of pictures yourself if you start to look for them in newspapers, magazines and comics. Start looking for pictures now and build up a collection.

Chapter 1 Norman Settlement

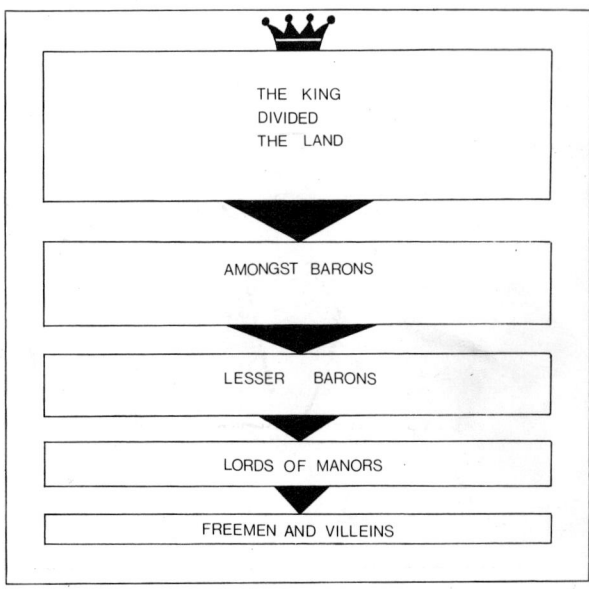

The Normans made certain that the Saxons could not shake off the rule of their conquerors. This land now owned by a Norman might well have belonged to a Saxon thegn before the battle of Hastings. Now it is guarded by a castle.

After Harold of Wessex had been killed at the battle of Hastings, William Duke of Normandy was able to crush any remaining English resistance to Norman rule because the English could not find another leader. William rewarded his followers with land, often taken from the English who had fought at the battle of Hastings. The most important posts in England now went to Normans. Norman earls were in charge of the very important border areas of Cheshire, Shropshire and Northumberland. A Norman became Archbishop of Canterbury and Norman clerks began to write out all important documents and laws in Latin. The Saxon villagers of England now found to their bitterness that their lord was one of the Norman conquerors.

THE KING DIVIDED THE LAND

AMONGST BARONS

LESSER BARONS

LORDS OF MANORS

FREEMEN AND VILLEINS

You will notice in this chapter how important land was. Remember that land was the main source of wealth at a time when money was not used as much as it is today.

William gave a lot of land to his chief men who in turn gave some of it to their followers and so on. Each man swore an oath of loyalty to the man who had given him land from the humblest person right up to the king as you can see in the diagram on the left.

Later on in his reign William decided to make everyone swear an oath of loyalty to the king as well as to the man immediately above him in the table opposite. This was to stop men from thinking that they only owed loyalty and military service to their landlord and not to the king as well.

Main changes
Most landowners were now Normans. The Normans spoke Norman French. They began to call the Saxon shires *counties*.
But:
The Saxon title of sheriff was still used for William's chief law officers.

William also decided to find out exactly how much land he himself owned in England and also to check on what everyone else owned. Also he wanted to find out what every man had to do in the way of services for the land he held. The picture shows you the clerks sent out by William getting the information which was written down in a great volume called Domesday book. You can still see it.

Types of services (rent) given in return for land.
1. Soldiers had to serve 40 days a year.
2. Peasants had to work on their lord's land at least three days in every week.

1. Complete the following sentences using the words in the box.
The English had no leader after _____ of _____ had been killed.
Important border areas in England were now under _____ earls.
Laws were now written in _____.
In return for land you swore an _____ of _____.
William sent out clerks to find out exact details of all land in England. They wrote this down in the _____ book.

> *Norman, Domesday, Oath, Harold, Loyalty, Wessex, Latin.*

2. Explain in your own words how the Normans established control in England.

3. Write down in your own words how the Domesday book was put together.

Getting the information for the Domesday book

Chapter 2 Knights

The knights who helped William I to win the Battle of Hastings looked like the one in the picture on the right. He is wearing a typical cone shaped Norman helmet with a nose protector called a **nasal** and his body is protected by a **hauberk**. This was a long leather coat covered in links of chain mail. Under the hauberk he would be wearing a long tunic of wool or linen and his legs are covered with thick stockings and leather cross-garters.

In battle Norman knights carried a lance and a long pear shaped shield. They also carried a heavy iron sword which was supported by a strap over one shoulder called a **baldric**. Knights were horse soldiers—that is what the word knight really means—and they always wore spurs. In time, spurs became the badge of knighthood and when a man became a knight he was said to have 'won his spurs'.

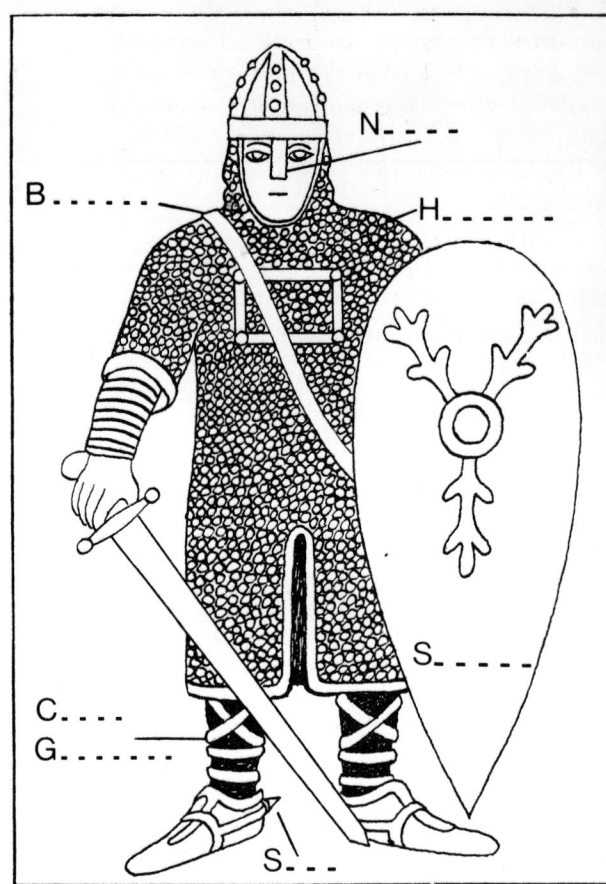

A Norman knight

1. Write a sentence about each of the following:
A Nasal
A Hauberk
A Baldric
Spurs

2. Draw the knight in the picture and fill in all the names.

The picture opposite shows why the knight's shield was pear shaped. It protected one side of his body when he was on horseback. It was wide enough at the top to protect his shoulders and narrow at the bottom to protect the knight's left leg.

3. Copy the picture into your book and write one or two sentences about the knight's shield.

The knight's shield

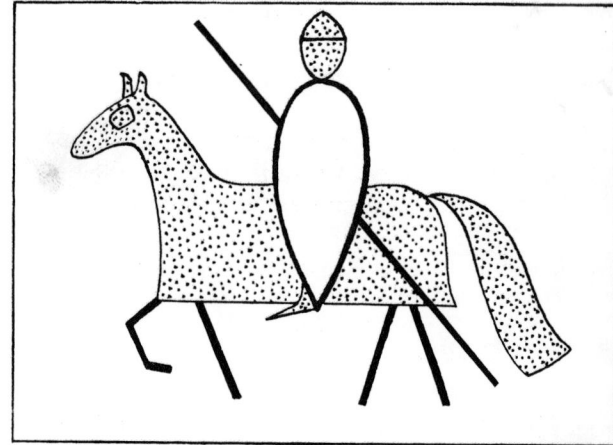

As time went on armour became more complicated. The links of chain mail were replaced by metal plates skilfully shaped to fit the knight's body by craftsmen called armourers. In the late Middle Ages, armour became so heavy that it was sometimes necessary to use a crane to lift a knight on to his horse. You can see this heavy plate armour in the picture on the right.

4. Complete these sentences, using the words in the box.

As time went on armour became more ____ .
Chain mail was replaced by armour made of metal ____ .
Armour was skilfully made by craftsmen called ____ .
In the late Middle Ages armour was so ____ it was sometimes necessary to use a ____ to lift a knight onto his horse.

> *Armourers, Crane, Complicated, Plates, Heavy.*

We always think of knights as soldiers because fighting was their main task, but they did have other duties too. Each knight received a grant of land from the king called his **fee**, which was a kind of payment for fighting in the king's army. Every knight was expected to look after his fee properly and act as Lord of the Manor. He also acted as a magistrate and held local courts and in addition he was expected to supply a fixed number of men-at-arms to fight in the king's army when they were needed.

5. On the right is a diagram showing all the knight's duties. Copy it into your book and write one or two sentences about it.

Plate armour

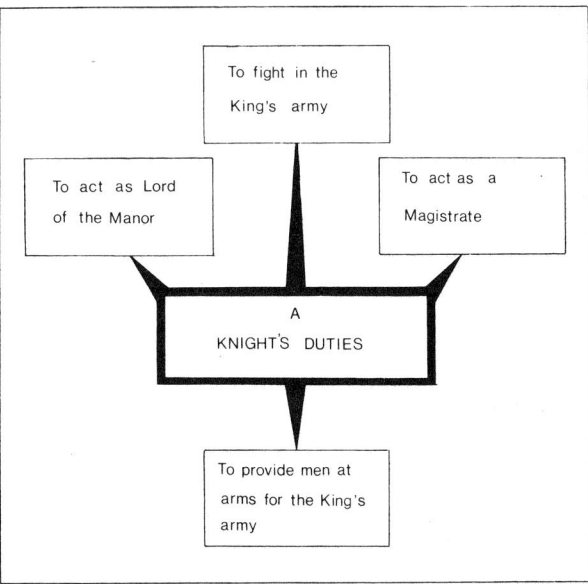

Chapter 3   Castles

Beaumaris castle in Anglesey.
This is one of the finest castles in Britain.

The word 'castle' comes from a Latin word meaning a fort. Important people who had the necessary power and money to build castles were able to get protection from their enemies. The Normans, as we have seen, wanted to be safe from the dangers of a Saxon rebellion. They quickly put up strong points which consisted of a mound of earth called a **motte**, and a courtyard called a **bailey**. On top of the motte was a tower or **keep** which was made of wood at first. Later the wooden keep was replaced by one made of stone. Another courtyard with extra walls and towers was added.

A motte and bailey castle

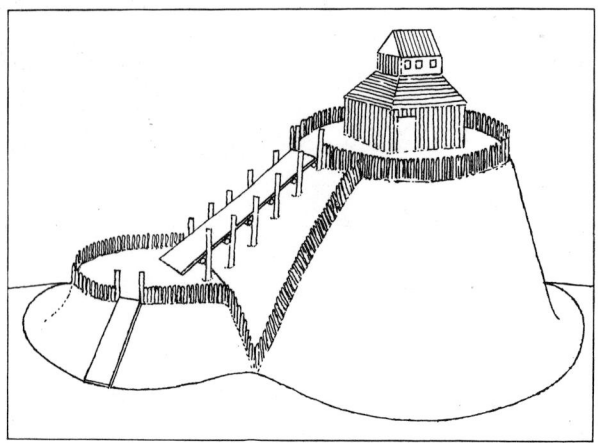

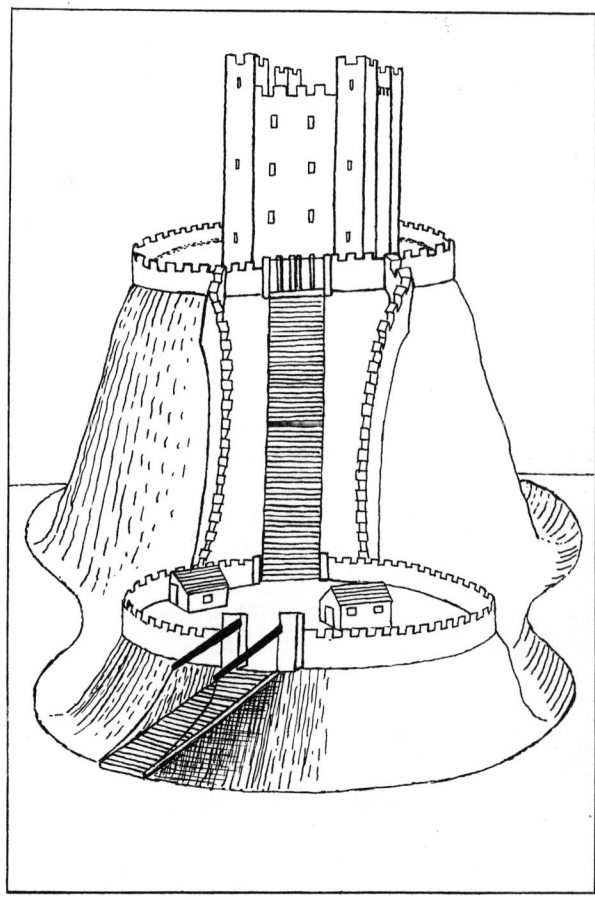

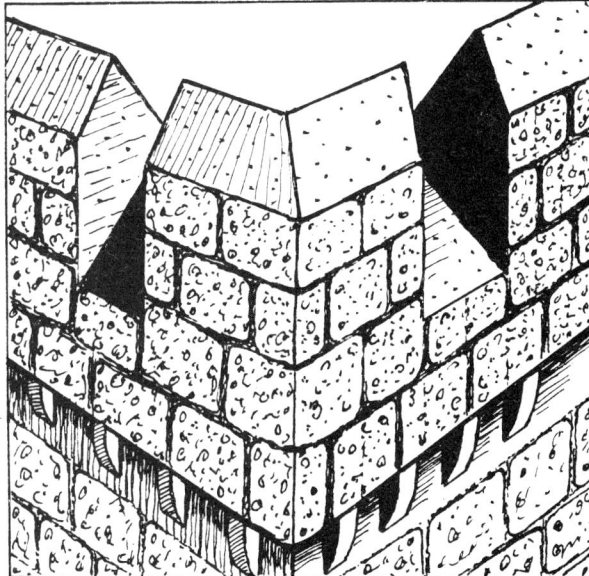

This castle shows the final stage of castle development. It has a very wide moat and the gateway has its own guardian building called a barbican.

The drawing above shows what castles looked like about three hundred years after the Normans came to England. Castles had to develop new styles of building in order to meet new methods of attack. In the castle above, soldiers in the towers would be able to shoot arrows at anyone trying to break down the walls of the castle in between the towers. The picture on the right shows you how the towers themselves were protected.

1. Complete the following sentences using the words in the box.

The Normans built ＿＿ and ＿＿ castles.

The ＿＿ was a courtyard.

The ＿＿ was a mound of earth.

The gateway was guarded by a ＿＿.

Motte, Barbican, Bailey.

Boiling oil or lead could be poured through openings in the overhanging part of the tower.

2. What sort of weapon would make castles out of date?

13

Chapter 4   Village Life

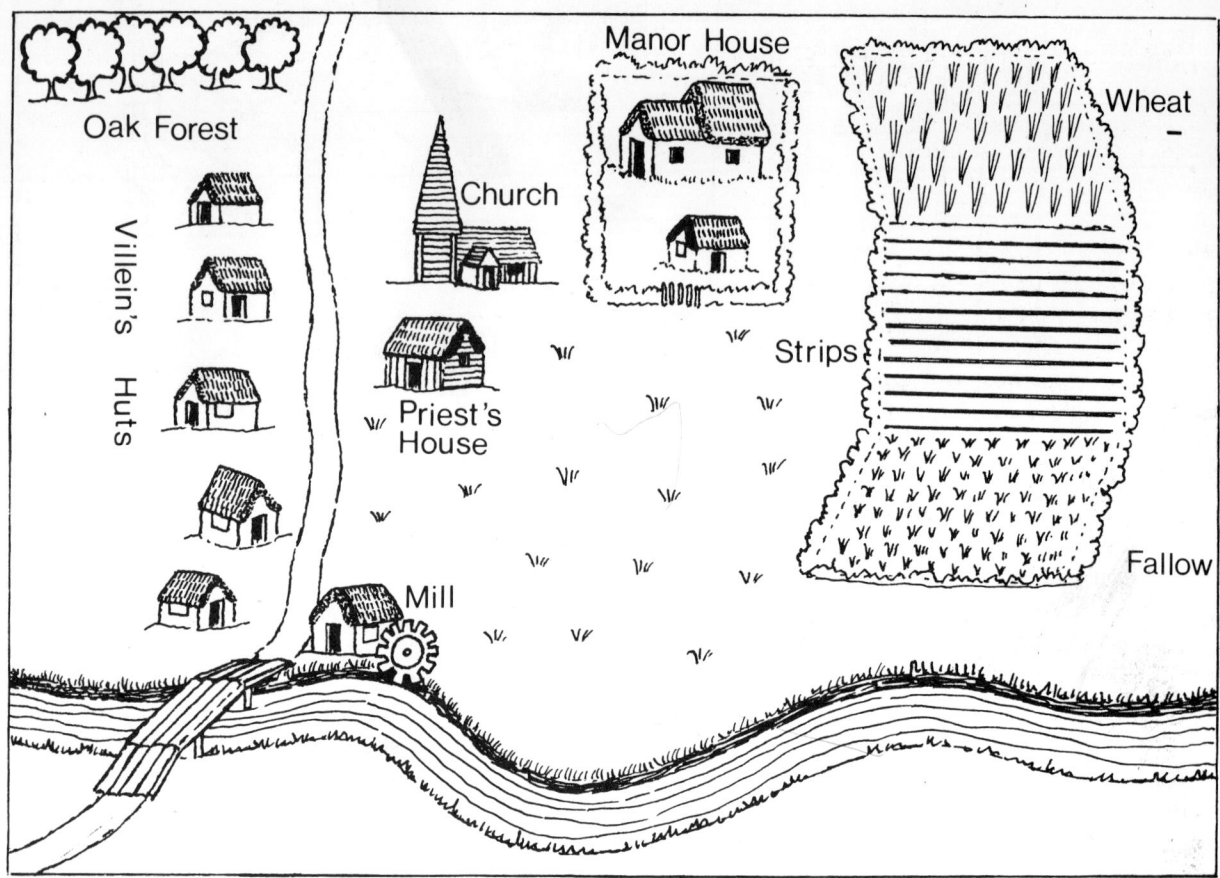

The village and its surrounding land used to look like this

There were very few towns in England at this time. Most people lived in villages known as manors (these included the land around the village). Sometimes there was more than one village in a manor.

Normans were now the lords of these manors —they were barons, knights or abbots of monasteries and the English peasants were known to them as **villeins** (people belonging to a village). The lord gave some land to the villagers as you can see in the diagram and kept the rest for himself. The villein promised to serve the lord with an oath of loyalty called **homage.**

In return for his land the villein had to work on the lord's land and supply him with food and other items.

If we rented land today we would pay in money not services.

The method of farming the land was much the same as in Saxon England. The land around a village was divided into three parts or fields. There were no hedges however. Instead each **open** field was divided into strips about 185 m in length and 18·5 m in width with a **baulk** of unploughed earth as a divider between the strips. A villein might have as many as 30 of these strips with some in each field because every year one field was not sown. It lay **fallow**—this gave each field a rest every third year.

The crops were wheat or rye, oats and barley. Peas and beans were sometimes grown in **crofts** of land around the homes of the villeins.

At special times, such as harvest, villeins were expected to do extra unpaid work for their lord. This was called boon work.

1. **How would the main crops be used?**

2. **What was the area of the strip?**

A villein was not free to move about as we are today. He could not leave his village without his lord's permission. He could not marry without permission. On the other hand his lord was expected to protect him.

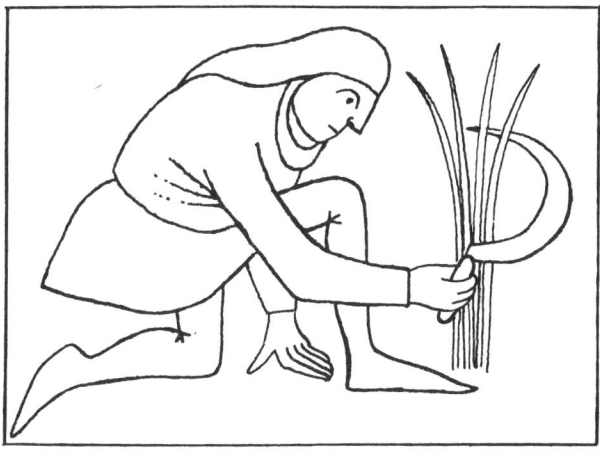

Villein service

3. **Complete the following sentences using the words in the box.**

The _____ were now the lords of the manor.
The villein had to swear _____ to his lord.
The **extra** work that the villein had to do on the lord's land was called _____ work.
The _____ and _____ looked after the lord's estates.
Strips were divided from each other by _____.

> *Homage, Boon, Bailiff, Baulks, Steward, Normans.*

Some villein services to his lord.

Three day's work a week on the lord's land.

Extra days at special times e.g. harvest work.

Eggs at Easter-time.

Hens at Christmas.

Pay at least one shilling if his daughter married.

A few villagers were freemen. Villeins wanted to be freemen also and a few were able to buy their freedom from a lord who might need money suddenly for some reason. Others ran away and perhaps became outlaws like Robin Hood or managed to escape to one of the few towns where if they could remain for a year and a day they were free.
If the villeins did not carry out their duties properly they had to go before the Manor Court to pay a fine. The lord's steward and bailiff saw to it that duties were carried out properly.

6. **Draw a picture of any two types of service that a villein had to carry out.**

4. **Sketch out a plan of the fixed system of crop rotation. The wheat crop was always followed by the oats and barley crop and then the field had a rest.**

5. **Why would the villeins particularly object to boon work?**

Chapter 5   Town Life

Although towns began to grow in size and in numbers after the Norman Conquest they were still very small by our standards.

The first aim of the townsfolk was to get a **Charter**, a document that gave them their freedom from the lord on whose land the town had grown up. This charter would give them the right to have a mayor and a law court of their own.

Lords of the manor were often very short of money so they would be glad to sell these rights to a town in order to help pay their debts.

The town would have a thick wall all round it to protect the people from enemies. You can see the walls in the picture above.

The streets were dirty, narrow and cobbled. Down the middle of the street a gutter or open drain ran. Refuse, manure, dead dogs and other unpleasant items found their way into this gutter. The little picture opposite shows the main water supply.

A medieval town, Conway in North Wales. *It is surrounded by well built walls and is also guarded by a fine castle.*

The water carrier

An old street in York called the Shambles. It was the butchers' street.

Shopkeepers often made their goods in their own houses and put them on display outside. Craftsmen working in a town joined a **gild**. There was a gild for each main occupation, goldsmiths, silversmiths, weavers, tailors, leatherworkers, vintners (wine sellers) and so on. The gilds fixed prices and standards of work. They collected money from their members and sometimes handed out sick pay and payments to widows of gild members. If you joined the gild you had to serve an apprenticeship before becoming a journeyman. Finally you made a **masterpiece** and became a mastercraftsman.

1. Explain in your own words the original meaning of the word masterpiece.

2. Complete the following sentences using the words in the box.

Townspeople bought the right to look after themselves by means of a ____.
Craftsmen in towns joined ____.
A craftsman had to serve an apprenticeship before becoming a ____ and finally a master.
Shopkeepers made their goods in their own

____.
Towns had thick ____ built around them for protection.

> *Gilds, Charter, Walls, Houses, Journeyman.*

Two shop signs

3. If you could see a medieval town you would notice that there were no pavements. No street lights. Pigs roaming about. You were fined 2p if your pig was allowed to wander. Make a list of the ways in which town and city life is better today. Are there any ways in which it is worse today than in medieval days?

4. Very few people could read in those days so shopkeepers used signs to show what they were selling. Can you decide what these two shopkeepers were doing for a living?

5. Think up some more possible signs and draw them.

Chapter 6   Monasteries

The ruins of Rievaulx Abbey

In the Middle Ages many people chose to live a strict religious life by becoming monks or nuns. They left the everyday world of their homes and families and went to live in great abbeys like the one at Rievaulx in North Yorkshire which you can see in the photograph. These buildings were very large and often housed several hundred people. Some of them are still in use, not as monasteries, but as cathedral churches in places like Durham, Chester and Gloucester, but many others have fallen into ruins. Even in their ruined state, however, it is possible to see how well they were planned and how skilfully they were built by the masons and craftsmen of the Middle Ages.

1. Complete these sentences, using the words in the box.

In the Middle Ages many people chose to live a strict religious life by becoming _____ or _____.

They went to live in great _____ like the one at _____ in North Yorkshire.

These buildings were large and sometimes housed several _____ people.

Some monasteries are still in use as _____ churches in places like _____, Chester and _____.

Some monasteries have fallen into _____.

It is still possible to see how well they were _____ and _____ by the craftsmen of the _____ Ages.

> *Abbeys, Nuns, Hundred, Durham, Monks, Cathedral, Planned, Gloucester, Built, Rievaulx, Ruins, Middle.*

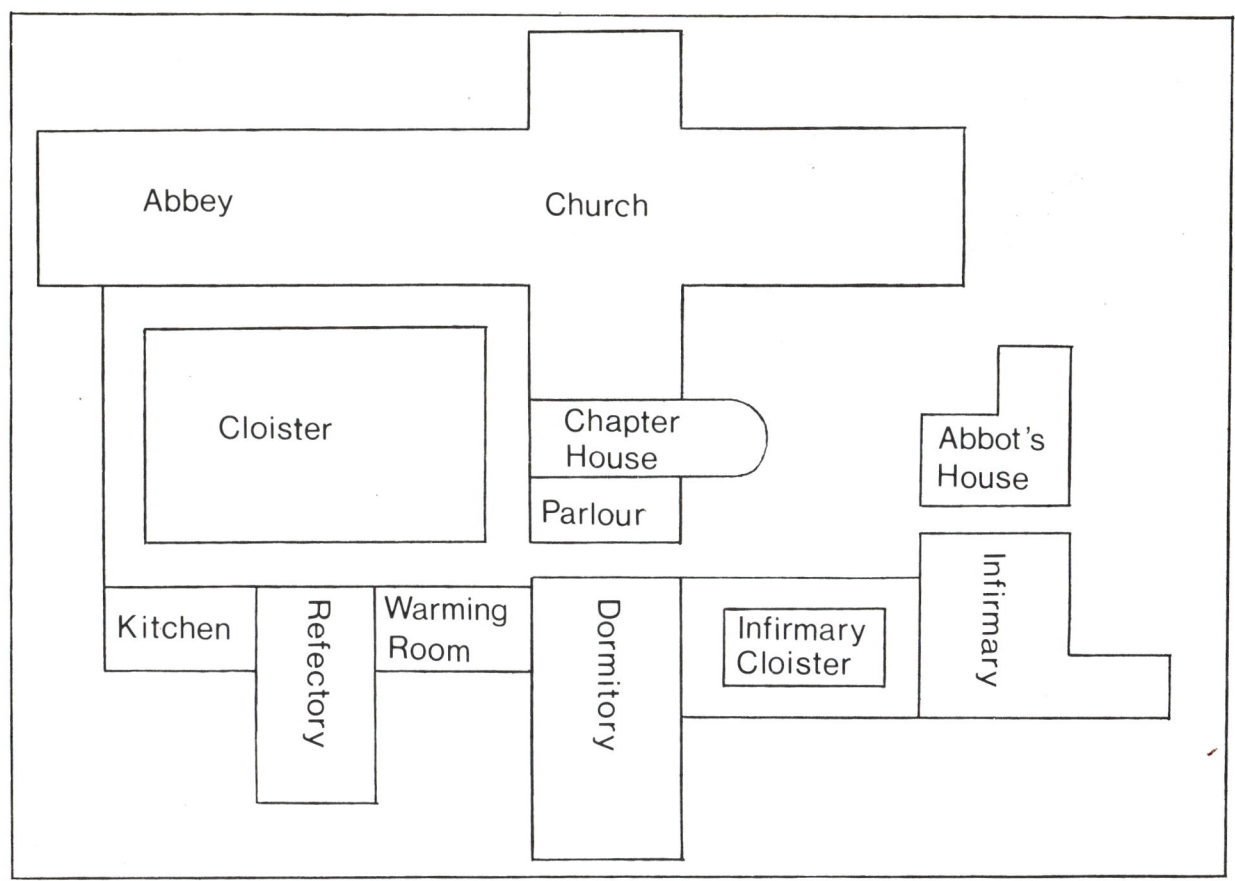

Ground-plan of Rievaulx Abbey

Here is a ground-plan of Rievaulx Abbey. At the top of the plan you can see the great abbey church which was always the largest building in a monastery. Next to the church are the cloisters, four covered corridors arranged in a square, and opening off the cloisters are the various domestic buildings. You can see the refectory where the monks had their meals, the dormitory where they slept and the kitchen where their food was prepared.

You can also see the chapter house where the monks met each morning to be given their tasks for the day and next to it the parlour where the monks were allowed to break their rule of silence and speak to each other. Nearby is the warming room or calefactorium where the monks were allowed to have a fire in winter and on the right hand side of the plan is the infirmary, the monks' hospital. The abbot who was the head of the monastery lived in a private house set apart from the rest of the abbey not far from the infirmary.

2. Draw the ground-plan of Rievaulx Abbey in your book and write in all the names.

3. Write a sentence in your book about each of the following abbey buildings.

The Abbey Church
The Refectory
The Dormitory
The Cloisters
The Chapter House
The Parlour
The Calefactorium
The Infirmary
The Abbot's House

Chapter 7 Monks and Friars

Life in the monasteries in the Middle Ages was far from easy. The monks lived by very strict rules, laid down by St. Benedict, which said that they must live in poverty, obey their abbot without question, and promise never to marry. The rules also said that they must devote themselves entirely to God and serve him through work and prayer.

The timetable of life in the monastery was designed to make sure that the monks lived in the way St. Benedict intended. They were called into the abbey church seven times each day for services and the rest of the day was strictly divided up into periods of work and study. Meals in the refectory were taken in silence while one monk read from the scriptures. This rule of silence was also enforced in the cloisters.

Every change of activity in the monastery was signalled by the ringing of the abbey bell which called the monks to the church, to their meals, to work and, finally, when the long day was over, to their hard beds and single blankets in the dormitory.

A monk

1. Complete these sentences, using the words in the box.

Monks lived by very strict ____.

The rules were laid down by St. ____.

The rules said that monks must live in ____, obey their abbot without ____ and promise never to ____.

The monks went into the church ____ times each day for services.

The rest of their day was divided into periods of ____ and ____.

> *Question, Work, Seven, Benedict, Rules, Study, Marry, Poverty.*

2. At the top of the page is a drawing of a monk. It shows his cloak called a habit, his hood called a cowl and his head shaven into a tonsure. On his feet he is wearing leather sandals. Copy the drawing into your book and write in the names.

Monks worked hard during the day in the monastery. Most of the morning was taken up with study and prayer but after lunch, which was usually served about midday, there was a period of work which lasted until about six in the evening. During this time, some monks worked in the fields growing food or tending sheep. Others worked in different parts of the monastery looking after the old and the sick, caring for travellers, or perhaps writing out manuscripts. Until the printing press was invented at the very end of the Middle Ages, all books were hand written and the monks were very skilful at copying and decorating the beautiful pages. The first letter on each page was usually illuminated and the monks often drew small pictures of their own everyday lives inside the letter. The one in the picture shows a monk at work.

An illuminated letter

3. Copy the picture of the illuminated letter into your book and colour it in.

4. Design an illumination on one of your own initials with a picture of part of your everyday life at school in it. Colour this drawing in too.

Not all men who wanted to live a religious life became monks. Some chose instead to become wandering friars. Friars dressed like monks and lived by rules which were just as strict but they did not live in monasteries. They believed they could serve God better by going out into the world preaching and healing the sick. The friars did much good work in the Middle Ages and they were greatly loved and respected. Simple lodgings called friaries were built in many towns in England and from these the friars went out each day to work among the people.

5. Write a few sentences about friars in your own words.

A friar preaching

Chapter 8   Houses

The Manor House at Stokesay in Shropshire

In the Middle Ages almost every village had its manor house where the lord, his family, and his household servants lived. These houses were very simple in design. The main hall, which was usually about fifteen metres long, occupied most of the building and here the lord would eat at a table placed on a small platform or dais at one end. Below the platform were the trestle tables at which the servants and soldiers had their meals and in the centre of the floor there would be an open hearth.

At the far end of the hall there were storerooms and over these the private bedroom and sitting room of the lord called the **solar**. The solar was usually reached by an outside staircase. The servants and soldiers slept in the main hall either on the floor or on the tables. Most manor houses were protected by high walls and some had strong towers for extra defence like the one you can see beyond the solar steps in the picture of the manor house at Stokesay.

1. Complete these sentences, using the words in the box.

In the Middle Ages almost every village had its ＿＿ house.

These houses were very simple in ＿＿.

The main hall was usually about ＿＿ feet long.

The lord would eat at a table placed on a small ＿＿ or dais.

Below the platform were the tables for the ＿＿ and soldiers.

In the middle of the floor there was an open ＿＿.

Manor houses were protected by high ＿＿ and sometimes by strong ＿＿ for extra defence.

Design, Towers, Manor, Servants, Hearth, Fifty, Walls, Platform.

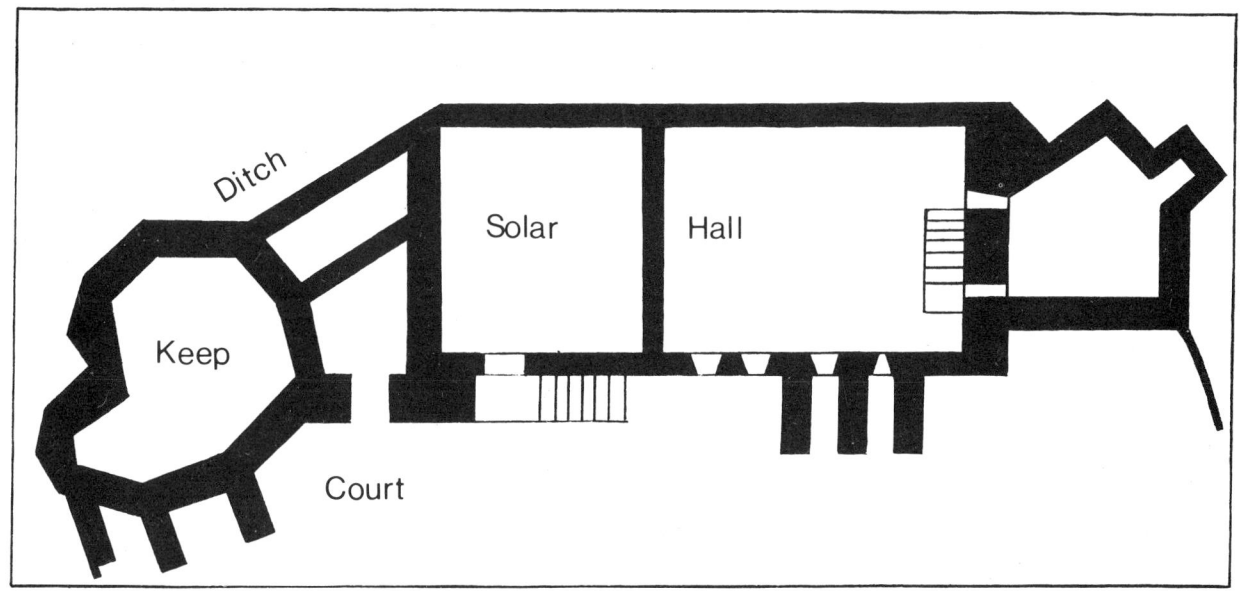

2. Here is a plan of Stokesay manor house. Copy it into your book.

3. Write a few sentences in your own words about manor houses in the Middle Ages.

Manor houses were usually made of stone, but ordinary people lived in simple wooden framed cottages. The roof was usually supported by two wooden beams called crucks and the walls were made of **wattle and daub**. Wattle is woven twigs and this acted as a foundation for the daub which was a mixture of mud and straw. Inside the cottages there would be a room for the family and stalls for the family animals. There were no windows, only wooden shutters, and usually no chimney. The smoke from the open hearth found its way out through a hole in the thatched roof. Life in these simple homes was very primitive.

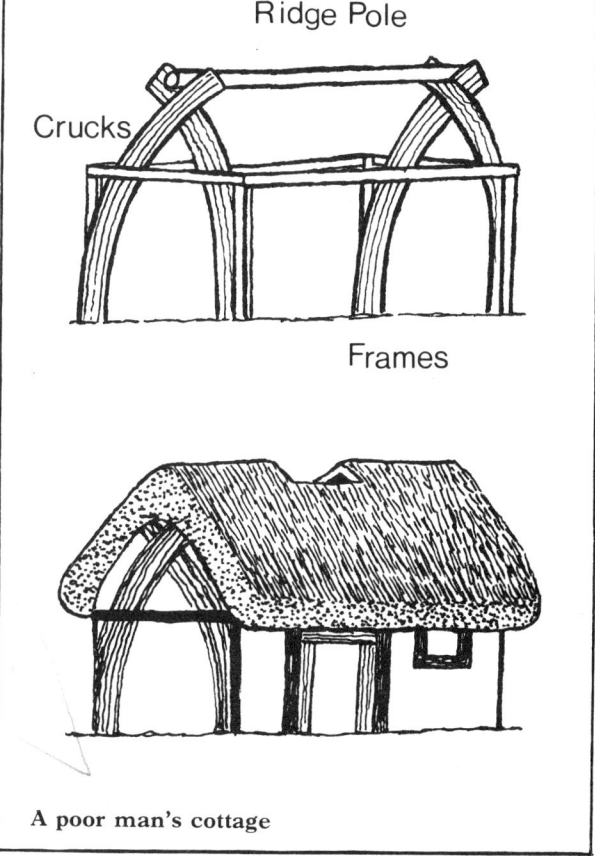

A poor man's cottage

4. Describe a poor man's cottage in your own words and draw the two pictures on the opposite side of the page.

Chapter 9   Everyday Life

Life in the Middle Ages was very different from life today. Few houses had windows, and furniture, even in the houses of the very rich, was extremely plain and simple. Carpets were rare and expensive and floors were often covered with rushes. There was no gas or electricity in those days, of course, and so rooms were lit by candles or flaming torches and food was cooked over open fires. The food was always very heavily flavoured with herbs and spices and was eaten in ways that we should find strange. It was sometimes served on large round slices of stale bread called **trenchers** instead of on plates and people used knives and their fingers to eat with because there were no forks. In wealthy households, **lavers** like the one in the picture on the right stood near the tables in the great hall so that pages could bring washbasins and towels to guests sitting at the table for them to wash their greasy fingers.

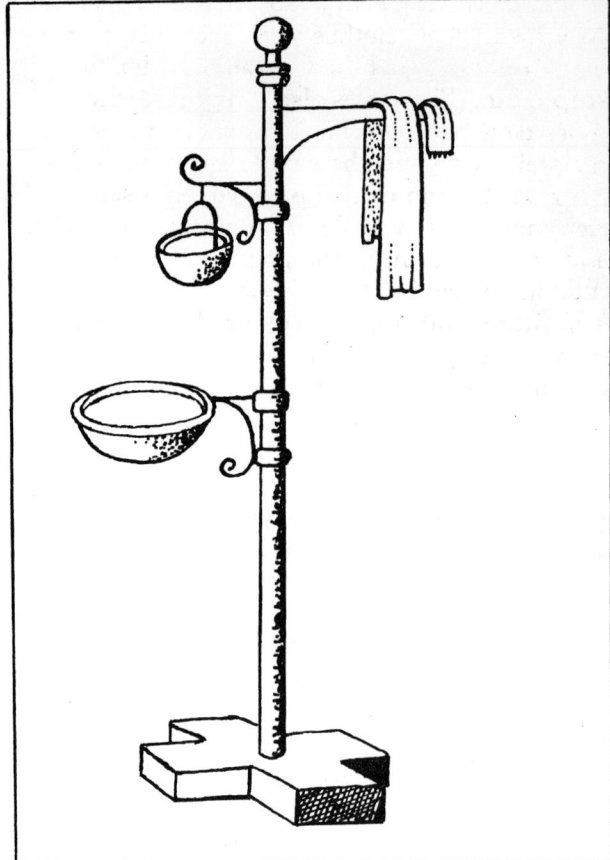

A laver

1. Complete these sentences, using the words in the box.

Life in the ____ ____ was very different from life today.
Few houses had ____ and furniture was extremely ____ and ____ .
Carpets were rare and ____ and floors were covered in ____ .
Rooms in the Middle Ages were lit with ____ or flaming ____ .
Food was cooked over open ____ .
The food was often served on large round slices of stale bread called ____ .
People ate with knives and their fingers because there were no ____ .
In wealthy households ____ stood near the tables in the great hall.

> *Trenchers, Middle Ages, Windows, Lavers, Candles, Fires, Forks, Torches, Plain, Expensive, Rushes, Simple.*

2. Draw the picture of the laver in your book and write two or three sentences about it.

The clothes people wore in the Middle Ages were also very different from ours. They did not have synthetic fibres such as nylon and terylene and they used very little cotton. Most clothes were made of wool or linen and rich people wore very heavy fabrics such as velvet. As a result their clothes were probably warmer than ours but much heavier and harder to keep clean. There was also a big difference in those days between the fashionable clothes of the well-to-do and the simple costume of the poor. At the top of this page you can see a rich man dressed in the costume of about 1100 and at the bottom of the page a poor man of the same period. The rich man's clothes are well fitting and brightly coloured. The poor man's clothes are loose and made from plain coloured material.

3. Write a paragraph in your own words about costume in the Middle Ages.

4. Draw the two pictures on this page in your book. Colour the rich man's clothes in bright colours and the poor man's clothes in dull colours.

5. Try to find some pictures of ladies' costume in the Middle Ages in your school library and draw and colour a rich woman and a poor woman of the same period. Write a few sentences about women's costume in your own words.

A rich man's costume 1100

A poor man's costume 1100

Chapter 10   Entertainment

Knights jousting. *From a modern film.*

Entertainments in the Middle Ages were often cruel and sometimes dangerous. Hunting and hawking were very popular and so too were cruel sports such as bear baiting and cock fighting. In addition many people enjoyed such dangerous pastimes as quarter staff fighting and jousting.

The knights who jousted by riding at each other with blunt lances were often seriously injured and sometimes people were actually killed. From time to time in the Middle Ages Popes gave orders that the knights of Europe should give up jousting altogether, but the sport was so popular that few knights took any notice. Jousts, like archery contests and other events which were regarded as a good training for war, continued throughout the Middle Ages and even on into Tudor times.

Hunting and ＿＿＿ were popular and so too were ＿＿＿ baiting and ＿＿＿ fighting.
Many people enjoyed such dangerous pastimes as ＿＿＿ staff fighting and ＿＿＿.
The knights who jousted rode at each other with blunt ＿＿＿.
Knights were often seriously ＿＿＿ in jousts and sometimes actually ＿＿＿.
From time to time ＿＿＿ gave orders that jousting should stop but few ＿＿＿ took any notice.

Dangerous, Quarter, Knights, Injured, Cruel, Jousting, Cock, Killed, Popes, Hawking, Bear, Lances.

---

1. Complete these sentences, using the words in the box.

Entertainments in the Middle Ages were often ＿＿＿ and sometimes ＿＿＿.

2. Why do you think jousts and archery contests were regarded as very useful in the Middle Ages?

Fairs were very popular in the Middle Ages but they were rather different from the fairs we go to. They were held in the trading towns once or twice a year and were really occasions for doing business. Merchants came from all over England and even abroad to buy and sell goods. Professional entertainers such as jugglers, acrobats and musicians used to visit the fairs as well, however, in order to amuse the crowds. As a result the fairs became places of entertainment as well as places of business. The townspeople themselves often put on plays and puppet shows during fair week and the tradition of some of these ancient fairs, for example the Nottingham Goose Fair, lives on into our own day.

3. Write a few sentences about a fair you have visited and say how it was different from the fairs in the Middle Ages.

4. Children in the Middle Ages enjoyed fairs just as you do. They also enjoyed many other games and pastimes. Use your school library to find out something about the following things and then write a few sentences about each one;

   Maypoles.
   Toys in the Middle Ages.
   Childrens' games in the Middle Ages.
   Football in the Middle Ages.
   Morris dancing.

If you look at a pack of playing cards you will see one card called a joker. In the Middle Ages jokers or jesters often entertained in the great halls or castles. Sometimes the jester was the comedian in a group of wandering minstrels who travelled from castle to castle giving entertainment. If a man was very wealthy he might have his own private jester. These men who were sometimes called 'fools' had the difficult job of trying to cheer up their master when he was miserable and good jesters could often be very cheeky. The witty remark of a 'fool' was often forgiven by a great lord who would punish anyone else for saying the same thing in a serious way. Some jesters in the Middle Ages had a lot of influence over the lord they served.

Morris dancing

5. In the picture below you can see a jester. Draw the picture in your book and write two or three sentences about jesters.

A jester

Chapter 11 Crime and Punishment

A modern actor in the stocks

There were no police forces or prisons in the Middle Ages such as we have today, but law and order was still maintained. In the villages one man was usually appointed to be village constable for a year in his spare time and everyone had the right to accuse a person suspected of a crime. When a man was accused there were law courts to deal with him. Judges representing the king travelled from town to town to hold assize courts and there were also local manor courts where the lord acted as the magistrate.

The church also had its own courts to deal with offenders and so wrongdoers did not go unpunished. The idea of trial by jury, in which twelve ordinary men listen to evidence and decide if a person is innocent or guilty, came into use in the Middle Ages at the time of King Henry II when the old Anglo-Saxon idea of trial by ordeal began to die out.

1. Complete these sentences, using the words in the box.

There were no ____ forces or prisons such as we have in the Middle Ages.
One man was usually appointed village ____ for a year.
When a man was accused there were ____ courts to deal with him.
Judges representing the ____ went from town to town to hold ____ courts.
There were also local ____ courts where the lord acted as ____.
The idea of trial by ____ came into use at the time of King Henry II and replaced the old Anglo-Saxon idea of trial by ____.

Law, Jury, Constable, King, Assize, Magistrate, Police, Ordeal, Manor.

Punishments in the Middle Ages were very harsh. The punishment was often made to fit the crime so if a man was convicted of stealing, his hand was cut off. If he was a murderer he was executed.

For smaller crimes the punishments varied. Sometimes people were fined or they might be sentenced to the stocks or the pillory. There they had to sit or stand, firmly locked in, while people stood and laughed and jeered at them or pelted them with rotten fruit. You can still occasionally see stocks standing in some villages today but they are no longer used, of course.

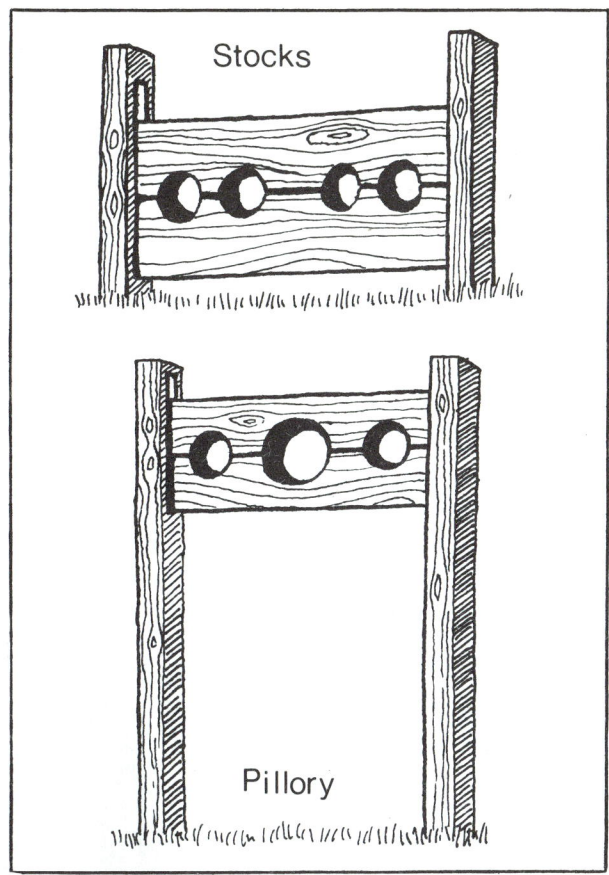

2. Write a few sentences about punishments in the Middle Ages.

3. Draw the stocks and the pillory in your books.

In the Middle Ages the gildsmen in the towns used to hold their own courts to punish members who had let the gild down by giving short weight or selling poor quality goods. We still use the phrase 'a baker's dozen', when we mean thirteen, because bakers in the Middle Ages used to put an extra loaf in each dozen to make sure they were not giving short weight. If they did, they were liable to be dragged off to the stocks on a sledge like the one in the picture with one of the loaves hung around their necks.

4. Draw the picture of the baker being punished in your book and write one or two sentences about it.

Chapter 12   Transport and Travel

A merchant travelling with a packhorse. *A rich traveller is going along with him. His lady rides on a pillion behind, the man on foot is a pilgrim. What was he doing?*

Going on a journey in medieval days was much more difficult than it is today. No one had built any new roads since the time of the Romans. You can imagine just how badly the Roman roads needed repairing. They had become tracks, dusty in summer and muddy in winter.

Many people walked to their destination. Wealthy people rode on horseback but carts were hardly ever used.

Merchants who had goods to move about used packhorses. It was their equivalent to our long distance lorries and freightliner trains. A journey could be very dangerous. The forests of those days often came right up to the edge of the roads and outlaws found travellers an easy prey.

1. Explain in your own words why laws were passed stating that the forest had to be cleared away from the edge of the roads.

A ship of the fifteenth century. *Notice the forecastle, the stern castle and the rudder. The lateen sail at the rear made it easier for the ship to steer against the wind. What do you think the forecastle and stern castle were for? Copy this drawing into your book.*

Ships were now becoming bigger. Merchants wanted to trade with other countries and more people began to want goods from abroad.

More sails were added and two, later three, masts became common. Instead of the vessel being pointed at both ends to make it reversible, a rudder was added.

It replaced the old Viking steering oar and it made it possible to turn the ship. The lateen sail made it easier to sail the vessel against the direction of the wind by tacking. The magnetic needle now began to be used to help in navigation.

2. Why was travel difficult in medieval days?

3. Complete the following sentences using the words in the box.

No one had built good roads in England since the ____.

Merchants moved goods about the countryside by means of ____.

The steering oar of a ship was replaced by a ____.

The ____ sail made it easier to sail against the wind.

Packhorses, Romans, Lateen, Rudder.

Chapter 13   Government

This copy of Magna Carta is in the British Museum

In 1215 a very unpopular King called John was ruling England. John had been fighting in France and had lost lands there that had belonged to the rulers of England.

John was desperately trying to raise money in order to go to war again and win back his lost lands. He made the great barons pay extra taxes and great fines that were unlawful. So the great landowners were angry with him.

John also angered the priests. He refused for a long time to agree to have the man they wanted as Archbishop of Canterbury. The leaders of the Barons and clergy met and drew up a list of demands or Charter which John was forced to sign at Runnymede. This Charter in Latin is known as Magna Carta, the Latin for Great Charter. John agreed to stop demanding extra taxes and unlawful fines from the landowners. He would take only what the laws allowed. He also agreed that all freemen should be tried in court by their equals and not just by the king or a king's judge and he made other promises which had the effect of giving away some of his power. The importance of Magna Carta is that it reminded John and other kings who followed him that a king of Britain does not have complete control over British people. Her monarchs have almost always had to share their power with someone else.

1. **What was the date of the signing of the Magna Carta?**

2. **What language was the Charter written in?**
Why was this language used?

3. **Who gained most from the Charter at the time?**

4. **Why did many people in England get no benefit at all from the Charter?**

Before the Norman Conquest the kings of England had to share power with a council of important men known as the **Witan**. The Norman rulers continued this idea and discussed important business with a meeting of lords and leading churchmen known as the Great Council. In time this Great Council came to be known as a **parliament** from a French word meaning 'to talk'.

In 1265 a powerful baron called Simon de Montfort decided to call a meeting of the Great Council and, because he wanted to get support for some of his plans from as many people as possible, he also invited ordinary knights from the shires and leading citizens from the towns to attend. In 1295 Edward I called a parliament which became a model for all future parliaments. He invited earls, barons, bishops and abbots to attend and also two knights from each county and two burgesses or leading citizens from each important town.

In later years so many men were collected together every time a parliament was called that it became necessary for some of them to occupy another building and so parliament divided. The earls, barons, bishops and abbots who were known as the Lords met in one place to hold their debates and the knights and burgesses, the Commons, met somewhere else. The king often acted as chairman of the debates in the House of Lords as he had in the days of the old Great Council but the men in the House of Commons had no chairman so they began to choose one for themselves. This chairman is known as the **Speaker** and ever since the Middle Ages right up to our own day debates in the House of Commons have been controlled by an official with this title.

The House of Commons is very much more powerful nowadays and really rules the country almost on its own. Nevertheless our Parliament still has many ancient traditions which go right back to the days of Edward and Simon de Montfort and the very first parliaments and these traditions, especially the one of allowing power in the country to be shared, are ones of which British people are very proud.

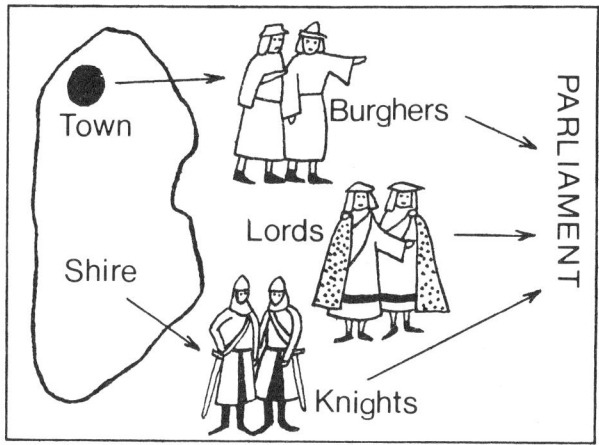

From 1295 onwards Parliament was organised like this.

5. Parliament's main job was to agree to the taxes needed by the King to run the country. How would this give Parliament a chance to gradually become more important?

6. What was the speaker's task? Who is the present speaker of the House of Commons?

7. Complete the following sentences using the words in the box.

Magna Carta was sealed at ____.
King John was trying to raise money in order to regain lands in ____.
Magna Carta said that a freeman was to be tried by his ____.
After the Norman Conquest kings had taken advice from the ____ ____.
Parliament was to consist of the lords, plus two ____ from every county and ____ ____ from every important town.

two burgesses, France, Runnymede, equals, knights, Great Council.

Chapter 14 Schools and Learning

Merton College, Oxford

Few people could read or write in the Middle Ages because there were very few schools. The great nobles thought more of war than they did of learning and so it was left to the church to provide what schools there were. Naturally the church was most interested in the training of priests and so the church schools taught mainly Latin grammar. That was the language in which church services were sung and in which the Bible was written. As a result these schools become known as **grammar schools.**

The grammar schools did not only train future priests, however. The sons of well-to-do merchants often attended them in order to get an education which would enable them to become better businessmen or perhaps enter the king's service as lawyers. Very ambitious boys went on from the grammar schools to the universities at Oxford and Cambridge which were founded in the Middle Ages. If you visit these university towns today, you can still see some of the beautiful college buildings which were put up at that time.

1. Complete these sentences, using the words in the box.

Few people in the Middle Ages could read or _____ because there were very few _____.
Schools were provided by the _____ and they taught mainly _____ grammar.
As a result they were called _____ schools.
Ambitious boys went on from grammar schools to the universities at _____ or _____.

> *Latin, Oxford, Write, Schools, Grammar, Cambridge, Church.*

The great scholars of the Middle Ages were theologians, men who studied religion, but there were also doctors, mathematicians and scientists. The scientists were chiefly interested in the stars and the planets and such things as the movement of the tides and they developed some of the earliest scientific instruments. One of these was called an **astrolabe** and it was used to measure angles and fix the position of the planets. Sailors still use a version of the astrolabe, called a sextant, to find their own position at sea.

2. Write a few sentences in your own words about scholars in the Middle Ages.

Towards the end of the Middle Ages the printing press was invented. This meant that knowledge could be spread more easily and more widely in printed books and printing was a most important discovery. The first English printer was William Caxton who set up a press in Westminster in 1476. Other presses followed in Oxford, St. Albans, and other towns and by 1500, at the very end of the Middle Ages, books were quite easy to buy.

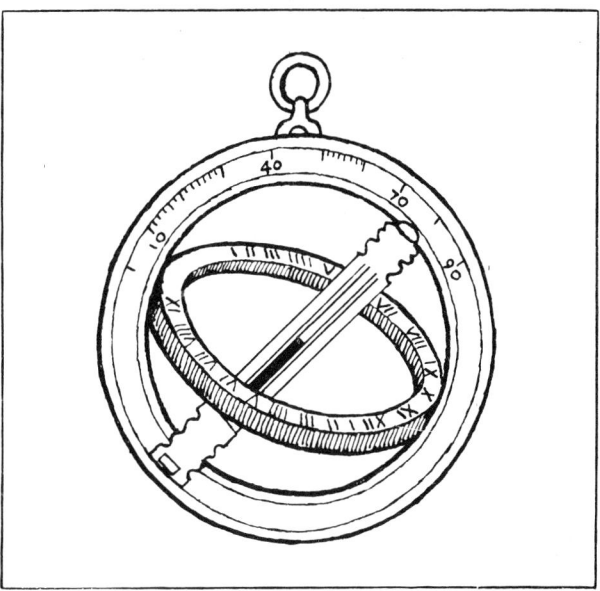

An astrolabe

3. Here is a picture of an astrolabe, draw it in your book.

4. Use your school library to find out more about William Caxton and his printing press.

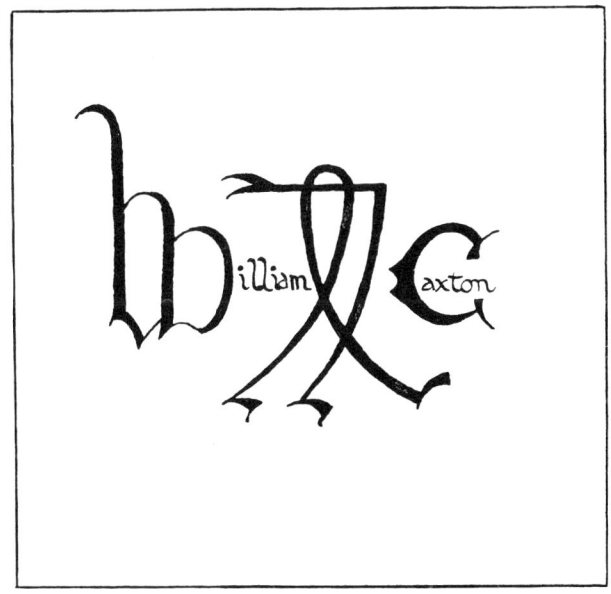

5. Here is William Caxton's trademark which he put in all his books. Copy it into your book.

Chapter 15 The Crusades

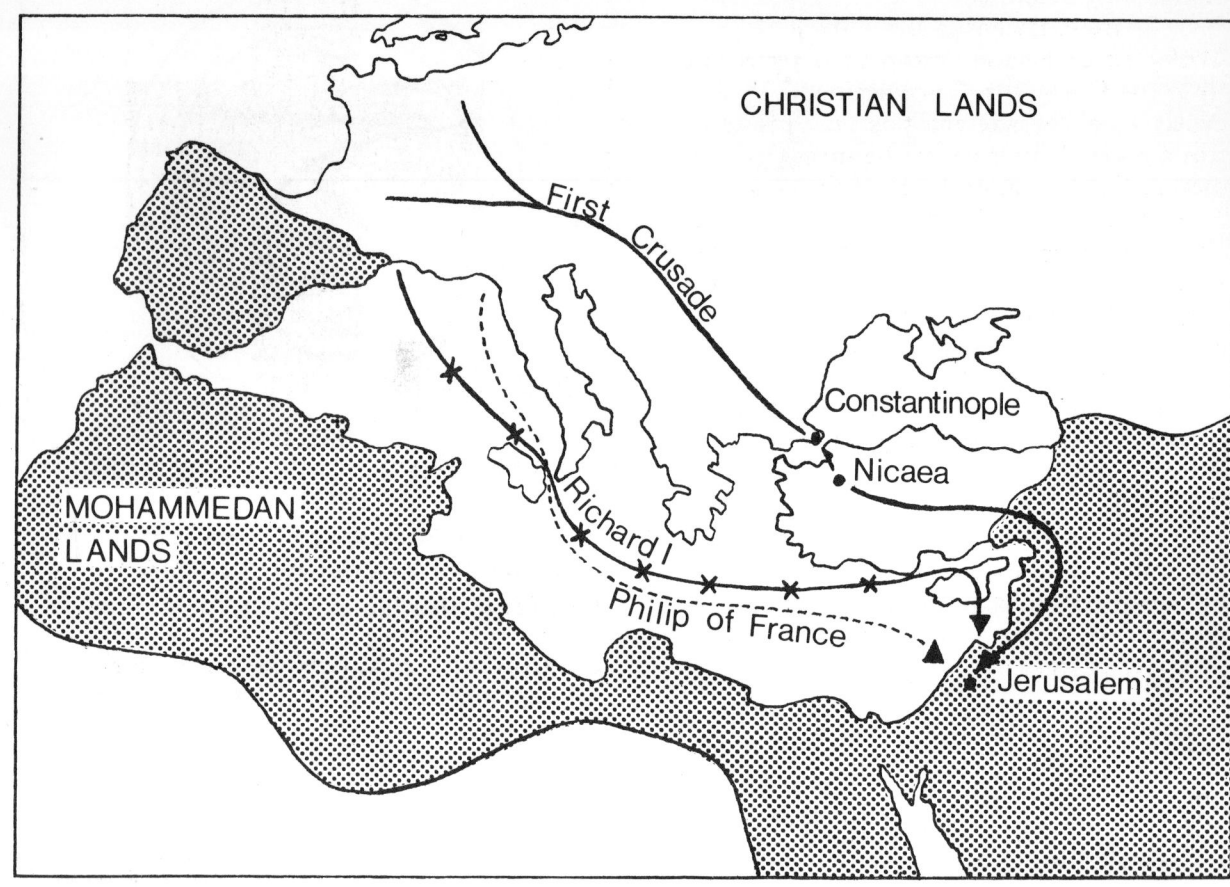

The Crusades

The word Crusade means holy war or War of the Cross and the idea of a Crusade was first preached by Pope Urban II in 1095. He called a great meeting of all the knights of Europe at Clermont in southern France and asked them to go on a Crusade to win back Jerusalem and the Holy Places in Palestine which had fallen into the hands of the Mohammedan Turks. Not only knights but also ordinary serfs led by a friar named Peter the Hermit left Europe in 1096 to make the long journey to Palestine. The badly organized army of serfs was massacred by the Turks at Nicaea but the knights, who were better prepared, were successful. They captured Jerusalem in 1099.

1. Complete these sentences, using the words in the box.

The word Crusade means ___ ___ or War of the ___.
The idea of a Crusade was first preached by Pope ___.
He asked the knights of Europe to win back ___ and the ___ ___ from the Mohammedan ___.
Not only knights but also serfs led by ___ the Hermit went on the Crusade.
The serfs were massacred at ___ but the knights were successful.

> *Urban II, Turks, Holy War, Peter, Cross, Nicaea, Jerusalem, Holy Places.*

After their victory, the Crusaders made the Holy Land into a Christian kingdom and many knights stayed there to build castles for protection and to farm great estates in the European fashion.

In 1187 the Saracens, a fierce tribe of Turks led by Saladin, recaptured Jerusalem from the Christians. Once again the Pope called for a Crusade and this time the call was answered by three of the most powerful men in Europe, King Richard the Lionheart of England, King Philip of France and the Emperor Frederick of Germany. Unfortunately the Crusade was not a success. The Emperor Frederick was drowned in a river on his way to the Holy Land and Richard and Philip quarrelled so badly that Philip took his army and went back home to France. Richard's army was not strong enough to attack Jerusalem on its own and so Richard and Saladin made peace. Richard agreed to leave the Holy Land and take his army with him and in return Saladin promised not to harm the Christian pilgrims who came to Palestine to visit the Holy Places.

2. Draw the map of the Crusades in in your book.

There were several more Crusades after the one Richard took part in but they were not successful. Many of the knights who went on the later Crusades were more interested in plunder than they were in fighting a Holy War and the jealous quarrels and greed of the Crusaders played right into the hands of the Turks. Jerusalem was never captured again by the Crusaders and the only really lasting result of the Crusades was the number of new things brought back to Europe by the knights who returned from the Holy Land. Rice, lemons, melons and apricots, cotton cloth, rugs and tapestries and eastern spices all became known in Europe as a result of the Crusades. So too did valuable knowledge and skills such as mathematics.

A Crusader's shield

3. Write a few sentences in your own words about Richard the Lionheart's Crusade.

4. Draw the picture of the Crusader's shield with its red cross badge in your book.

5. Below is a drawing of one of the things the Crusaders brought back to Europe. Copy it and then make a series of drawings of your own to show the other things they brought.

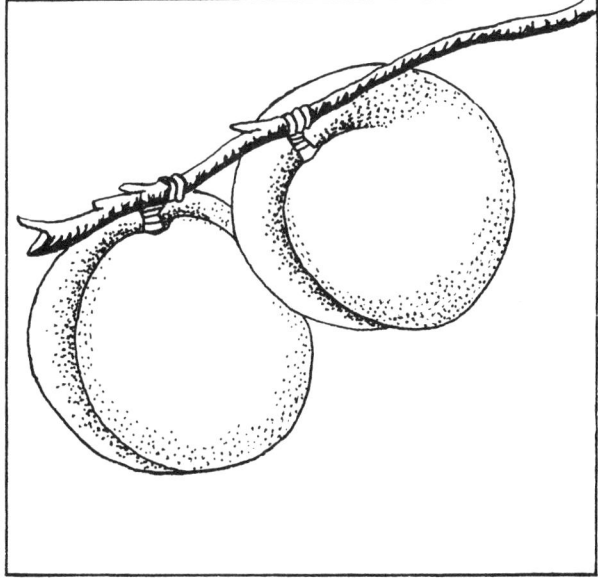

Apricots

Chapter 16   Battles

Knights at the Battle of Agincourt. *From a modern film.*

Battles in the Middle Ages were fought between armies of mounted knights, supported by foot soldiers called men-at-arms. The first shock of attack was usually a charge by the knights who tried to cause panic in the enemy ranks. If they succeeded the men-at-arms followed up to drive the enemy back in fierce hand to hand fighting with swords. As time went on the English began to make greater use of archers who rained down their arrows on the enemy soldiers.

The English longbow was made of yew and it was amazingly powerful. Arrows from a longbow could pierce chain mail and knights began to wear the much heavier plate armour in order to protect themselves. The English and the Welsh archers were the most famous longbowmen in Europe but other countries relied more on the crossbow which was not as powerful but was easier to use.

1. Complete these sentences, using the words in the box.

Battles in the Middle Ages were fought between armies of mounted _____.

The first shock of an attack was usually a _____ by the knights.

The knights were supported by foot soldiers called _____.

As time went on the English began to make greater use of _____.

The English longbow was made of _____ and was amazingly _____.

The arrows from a longbow could even pierce _____ _____.

The _____ and the _____ were the most famous longbowmen in Europe.

Yew, Knights, Men-at-Arms, Archers, Chain mail, Powerful, English, Charge, Welsh.

Capturing a castle was a most difficult task in the Middle Ages and all sorts of strange machines were invented to make the job a little easier. Huge catapults called **mangonels** were used to hurl heavy stones against castle walls and even bigger machines called **trebuchets,** like the one in the picture on the right, threw dead and rotting animals over the castle walls to cause disease among the defenders inside.

When the attackers thought the castle garrison was weak enough through disease and starvation, scaling ladders and siege towers, like the one at the bottom of the page, were used to make a direct attack. Men scrambled up the ladders and jumped off the siege tower on to the walls of the castle to take it by storm.

All the time the attackers were fighting to get inside the castle the defenders would be using boiling water, oil and tar to keep them out. The men manning the walls would try to push the tall scaling ladders down and set set fire to the siege tower. You can see in the picture that the siege tower is covered in skins which were soaked in water to try to stop the tower from catching fire. In the later Middle Ages, after gunpowder had been invented, methods of attack began to change and castles ceased to have so much value.

A trebuchet

2. Describe the methods used to attack a castle in your own words.

3. Draw the trebuchet and the siege tower in your book.

4. Try to find a picture of a mangonel and some information about it to put in your book.

5. Why do you think the invention of gunpowder changed methods of attack?

A siege tower

Chapter 17   Wales and Scotland

![Caernarvon Castle]

Caernarvon Castle. *One of the fortresses built by Edward in Wales.*

Edward I of England, the grandson of King John, also wanted to become ruler of Wales and Scotland.

The map shows you how the Welsh had been able to remain independent in the mountains of Wales. Sometimes they raided across the English Border despite the strong castles built to guard the people living near the border. Edward decided to end this raiding by conquering all Wales.

He trapped the Welsh leader Llewelyn in the mountains of Snowdonia and prevented any food from reaching him by placing his soldiers at the entrances to the mountain passes and by patrolling the Menai Straits with his ships.

Llewelyn surrendered but rebelled later with his brother David-Llewelyn and was killed, David was executed and Edward built strong castles in Wales. He also tried to please the Welsh by naming his baby son Prince of Wales.

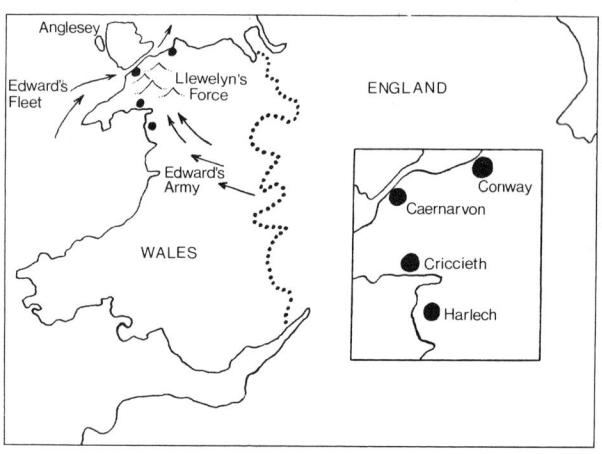

Wales. *Notice the mountainous part and the castles built by Edward.* **Copy out the map carefully in your books. Make a list of the castles built by Edward to guard his new possessions.**

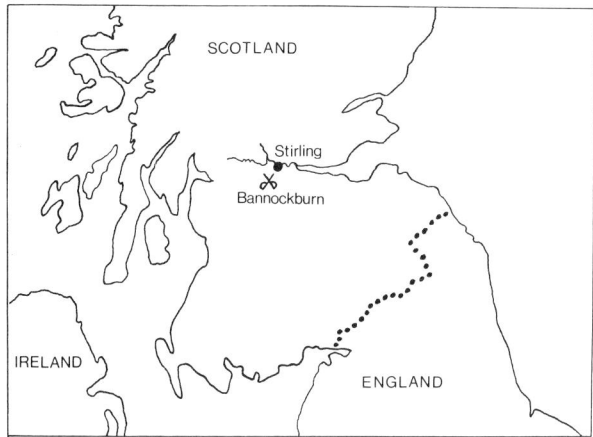

Scotland. *Notice the important position of Stirling Castle.*

Fighting on the border between Scotland and England had gone on for centuries. Edward I was determined to end that as well.
The Scots gave him a chance to interfere in Scotland when he was asked to choose the King of Scotland from thirteen candidates. Edward chose one who would agree to do homage to him as his overlord.
William Wallace rallied the Scots against the English but he was defeated and executed. The four quarters of his body were put on show in Scotland.
Edward II the next English King was not as warlike as his father. Robert Bruce now led the Scots and began to drive the English out of Scotland. When Bruce threatened Stirling Castle Edward II came to the rescue with a large army but also was crushed at the battle of Bannockburn. The Scots were free from English Rule.

1. Complete the following sentences using the words in the box.

Edward I was king of ____ but he also wanted to rule over ____ and ____.
The leader of the Welsh was ____.
The Welsh stronghold was in the mountains of ____.
The Scots were led to victory against the English by ____ ____.
The great Scottish victory was at ____.

> *Scotland, Llewelyn, Bannockburn, Snowdonia, England, Wales, Robert Bruce.*

2. At the battle of Bannockburn the Scots trapped some of the heavily armoured English knights by digging pits in front of the Scottish lines and lightly covering them over. Describe by words and pictures what would happen when the English knights rode into these traps.

3. What were Edward's reasons for attacking Wales and Scotland?

4. What was Edward's excuse for interfering in Scotland?

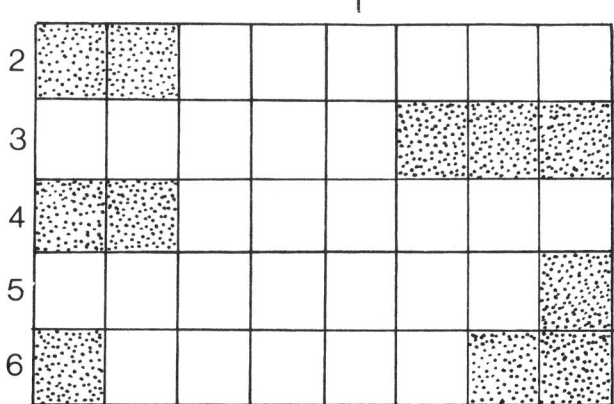

1. Straits patrolled by Edward's ships.
2. What you had to do to your overlord in return for land.
3. Leader of the Scots at Bannockburn.
4. Welsh Castle.
5. Scottish leader cut into quarters.
6. Llewelyn's brother.

Chapter 18 Plague and Rebellion

The Black Rat: The cause of the spread of the Black Death
From an early engraving

In 1348 England was attacked by a terrible disease called the Black Death. This disease was the bubonic plague and there were outbreaks of it from time to time. But on this particular occasion many thousands of people died. It came from China and was spread by black rats and merchants' goods coming from the East.

The victims developed darkish boils. Other signs were great sweating and violent sneezing. Death sometimes came within a day of these signs appearing. As the disease spread rapidly in the dirty and insanitary living conditions of the time, the poorer people suffered very badly. Many priests also died because of the help they gave to the dying.

The survivors of the Plague found that there were now more jobs than men to do them.

Villeins (who were not freemen) saw a chance to become free by slipping away to work for anyone who would offer them freedom to work for a wage instead of the old duties such as ploughing and reaping. Freemen who already worked for money wanted more.

There was great anger and discontent when Parliament passed a law saying that wages must not go above the rate paid before the Black Death and that all peasants ought to be villeins and not freemen.

1. What type of person would be in Parliament in those days? Your answer should help to explain the last paragraph above.

The discontented peasants became even more angry in the years after the Black Death. The cost of wars with France mentioned in the next Chapter caused taxes to go up. They always fell most heavily on the poorest. John Ball, a priest, went round the countryside saying that things would not get better until all men were equal. Then, in 1381, a Poll Tax (one on every head) of a shilling was put on everyone. This was a day's pay for a villein. Wat Tyler led a rebellion of furious peasants from Kent. Others rebelled in Essex and other parts of England. The Kent and Essex rebellion broke into London. They sacked the great Savoy Palace and killed the Archbishop of Canterbury and the Royal Treasurer.

When the angry peasants were storming through London burning and killing, England was ruled by Richard II, a fourteen year old boy. The fact that a boy king was on the throne probably gave the peasants confidence because they expected him to be weak and timid, but in fact they were very much mistaken. It was Richard's bravery which brought the revolt to an end.

He decided that he ought to meet the rebels and talk to them. So he left the safety of the Tower of London and rode out to Smithfield Market to meet Wat Tyler face to face. Tyler was so rude to the king that the Lord Mayor of London knocked the peasant leader to the floor where he was stabbed to death. Immediately the peasants saw this they shouted with anger, but Richard did not back away. Instead he rode forward and told the peasants that he was now their leader and that if they trusted him he would give in to their demands. This brave act impressed the peasants so much that they cheered the king and agreed to go back home. Sadly, Richard did not keep the promises he had made. The other leaders of the rebellion, like John Ball, were hunted down and hanged and the conditions of the peasants in the countryside did not really improve as a result of the rebellion. When improvements did come, they came gradually and not in the dramatic way that Wat Tyler and his followers had hoped for.

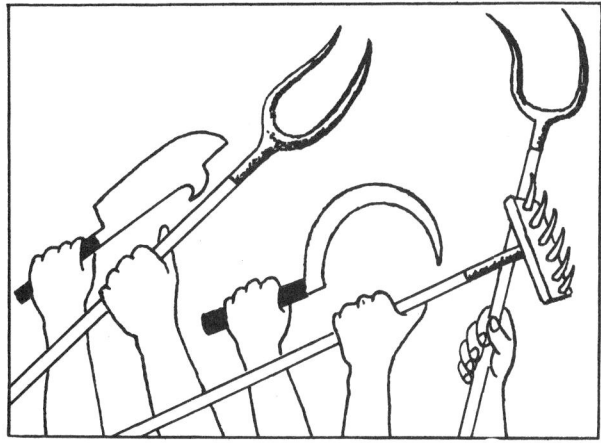

The rebels in London

2. When Adam delved and Eve span who was then the gentleman? This was John Ball's message to the people. What did it mean?

3. Make a list of reasons for the Peasant's Revolt.

4. Describe the meeting between Richard II and the peasants at Smithfield in your own words.

5. Complete the following sentences using the words in the box.

The Black Death was spread by ____ ____.
The peasants who survived the Black Death wanted ____ and higher ____.
The peasants objected to paying the ____ tax.
The rebellious priest was ____ ____.
The leader of the Kent Rebels was ____ ____.
Promises of freedom were signed by ____

____.

> *Black rats, King Richard, Wages, John Ball, Freedom, Wat Tyler, Poll.*

Chapter 19 The Hundred Years War

![The Battle of Agincourt 1415]

The Battle of Agincourt 1415. *From a modern film.*

When Edward III attacked France it started a war that went on for over a hundred years. There were a number of reasons for this war. French and English sailors fought each other off the south coast of England. English wool merchants complained that French officials tried to stop them sending wool to Flanders. The French often helped the Scots in their wars against England.

After the fighting had started, Edward claimed that he had the right to be king of France. You can work out his claim from the diagram below. Edward probably did not take this claim very seriously. It was just a good excuse.

The English won some fine victories thanks to their archers and the longbow. It was the deadliest weapon in Europe, being about two metres in length and made of yew. Its hempen string had to be drawn right back to the ear. Such a bow needed the strength of the whole of the archer's body not just his arm in order to loose off the one metre arrow which was usually made of ash with goose feathers.

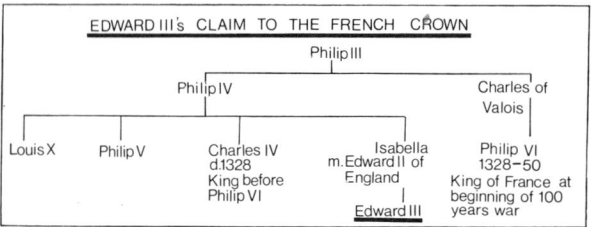

EDWARD III's CLAIM TO THE FRENCH CROWN

Philip III

Philip IV — Charles of Valois

Louis X — Philip V — Charles IV d.1328 King before Philip VI — Isabella m. Edward II of England — Philip VI 1328–50 King of France at beginning of 100 years war

Edward III

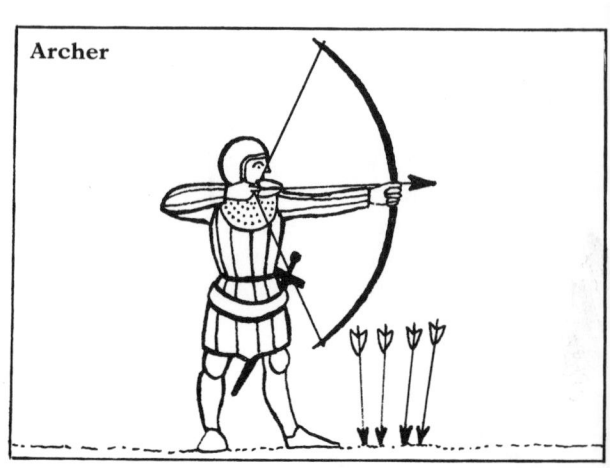

Archer

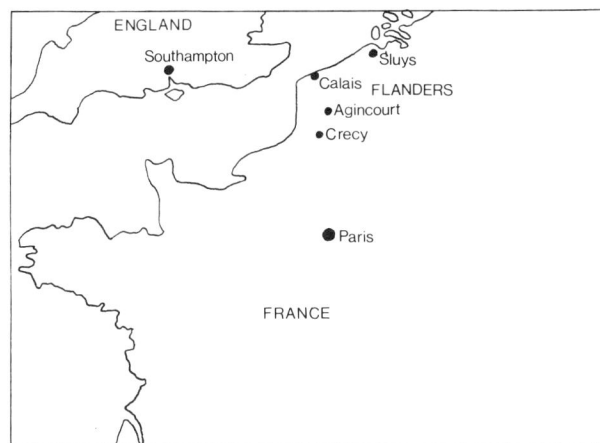

France during the Hundred Years War

First of all the English defeated the French at sea in the battle of Sluys. Then in 1346 Edward III won a great victory at Crecy against a much more powerful French army. The French were slaughtered by the English longbowmen. Edward captured the important port of Calais.

The French learned to avoid big battles where they were exposed to longbow fire. Gradually they regained most of what they had lost until, at Agincourt in 1415, Henry V crushed the French who were fighting as a large army. Henry V died soon after this and the French were rallied by a girl, Joan of Arc. Although she was captured and burnt by the English, the French were able to go on and clear the English out of all France except Calais.

The French found the cannon an answer to the longbow. It could destroy the longbowmen from a distance.

1. Complete the following sentences using the words in the box.

The English ___ merchants complained that their trade was being interfered with by the French.

The title of King of France was claimed by ___ .

The first great English victory on land was at ___ .

The English gained the very important port of ___ .

The French found an answer to the English longbow by using ___ .

The French found a leader in ___ .

Calais, cannon, Edward III, Joan of Arc, Wool, Crecy.

2. Make a list of the reasons for war between the French and the English.

3. Copy the map into your book and underline the English victories shown on it, also the port captured by the English.

4. Copy out the diagram of the archer. Name the materials and give the measurements of the bow and arrow.

Chapter 20 The Wars of the Roses

Richard III

Henry VI, who came to the throne in 1422, was a weak and feeble king and during his reign the great barons were constantly fighting among themselves to gain more wealth and power. When Henry went mad in 1453, the quarrels turned into a full scale civil war.

Henry was head of the Lancaster family and his supporters, whose badge was the red rose, fought to keep Henry on the throne. Their rivals were the followers of the house of York, whose badge was a white rose. They said that Henry was unfit to be king and they wanted to remove him and make their own leader, the Duke of York, king in his place.

The first round was won by the Yorkists and in 1461 Henry was pushed aside to make way for Edward Duke of York who became King Edward IV. Then, in 1470, the Lancastrians were successful and Henry VI became king again for a few months. In 1471, however, he was murdered and Edward IV came back to the throne and ruled until his death in 1483.

1. Complete these sentences, using the words in the box.

Henry VI was a weak and feeble king and during his reign the _____ were constantly fighting.

In 1453 Henry went _____ and the quarrels turned into a _____ war.

Henry was head of the Lancaster family whose badge was a _____ rose.

The badge of the Yorkists was a _____ rose.

The Yorkists won the first round and _____ Duke of York became king.

When he died his twelve year old son became _____ but he was murdered by his _____ Richard Duke of Gloucester.

> *Mad, Uncle, White, Edward, Red, Edward V, Barons, Civil.*

The next king was Edward's twelve year old son who became Edward V but he did not even reign long enough to be crowned. The boy king and his younger brother were imprisoned and then murdered in the Tower of London by their uncle Richard Duke of Gloucester who took the throne for himself and became King Richard III.

King Richard III did not reign for very long. The murder of his two nephews made him as unpopular with his own Yorkist followers as he was with the Lancastrians and his enemies united against him and found a leader in Henry Tudor Earl of Richmond, a Lancastrian. Henry defeated Richard in battle at Bosworth Field in 1485 and he became king himself. The legend is that Henry found Richard's crown in a thornbush after the battle and placed it on his own head to become King Henry VII.

2. Write a few lines in your own words about Richard III.

Henry VII did not allow the Wars of the Roses to continue. He married Elizabeth of York in order to unite the Lancastrian and Yorkist families and the two badges were placed together to make the Tudor rose. He put down the power of the barons and taught them to respect the king's laws. Under his wise rule, at the very end of the Middle Ages, England became a peaceful country and the foundations were laid for the great Tudor Age which you will learn about next.

3. Draw the three badges which you can see on this page and colour them in correctly.

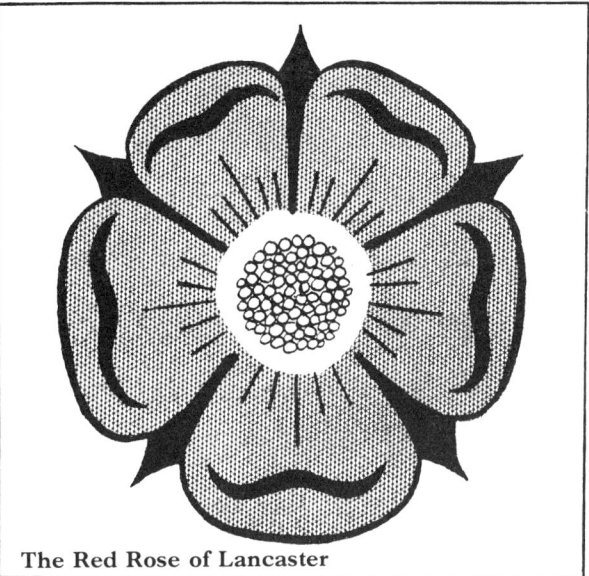

The Red Rose of Lancaster

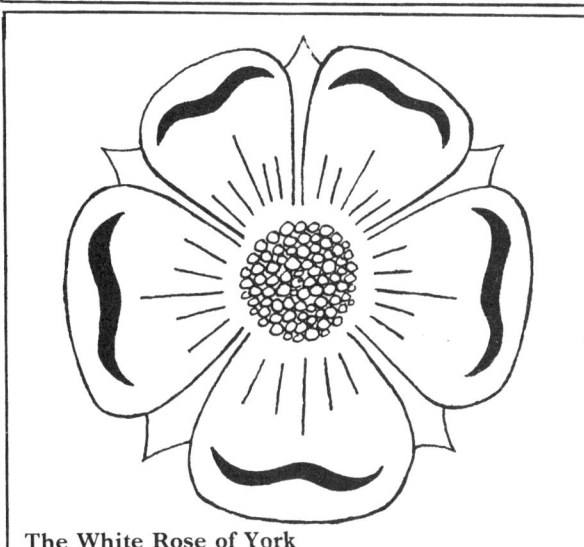

The White Rose of York

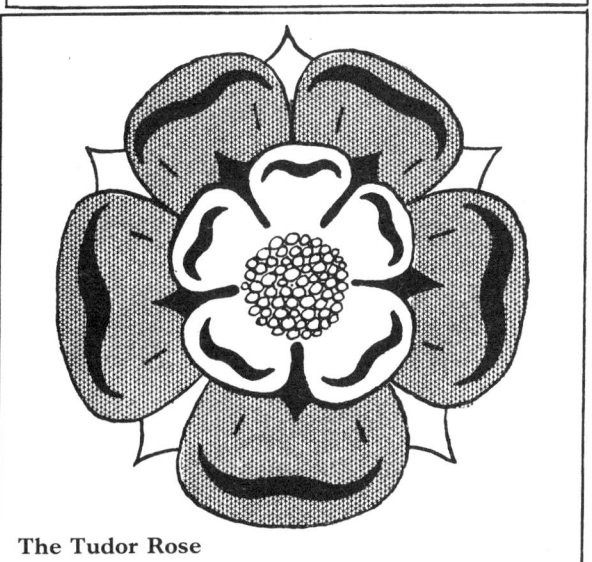

The Tudor Rose

To the teacher

The chapters in this book have been designed to provide a simple outline course in the history of the Middle Ages but it is not intended that they should be used in isolation. Most teachers will wish to enlarge upon the information they contain by showing their classes films and pictures, by using radio and television broadcasts and by arranging visits to museums and historical sites. They may also wish to encourage their classes to make models of some of the items mentioned in the text.

The history of the Middle Ages can also be a fruitful starting point for imaginative work in art and written English and teachers who take slower learning classes for a combination of subjects such as English, history, geography and art would find the Middle Ages a valuable theme for a full term's integrated work. There is a great deal of excellent children's fiction based on the Middle Ages by Henry Treece, Geoffrey Trease and others which can be used in both history and English lessons.